THE CENCI—1598

by

Alexandre Dumas

British Library Cataloguing-in-Publication Data
A catalogue record for this book is available from the
British Library

Alexandre Dumas

Alexandre Dumas was born in Villers-Cotterêts, France in 1802. His parents were poor, but their heritage and good reputation – Alexandre's father had been a general in Napoleon's army – provided Alexandre with opportunities for good employment. In 1822, Dumas moved to Paris to work for future king Louis Philippe I in the Palais Royal. It was here that he began to write for magazines and the theatre.

In 1829 and 1830 respectively, Dumas produced the plays Henry III and His Court and Christine, both of which met with critical acclaim and financial success. As a result, he was able to commit himself full-time to writing. Despite the turbulent economic times which followed the Revolution of 1830, Dumas turned out to have something of an entrepreneurial streak, and did well for himself in this decade. He founded a production studio that turned out hundreds of stories under his creative direction, and began to produce serialised novels for newspapers which were widely read by the French public. It was over the next two decades, as a now famous and much loved author of romantic and adventuring sagas, that Dumas produced his best-known works – the D'Artagnan romances, including The Three Musketeers, in 1844, and The Count of Monte Cristo, in 1846.

Dumas made a lot of money from his writing, but he was almost constantly penniless as a result of his extravagant lifestyle and love of women. In 1851 he fled his creditors to Belgium, and then Russia, and then Italy, not returning to Paris until 1864. Dumas died in Puys, France, in 1870, at the age of 68. He is now enshrined in the Panthéon of Paris alongside fellow authors Victor Hugo and Emile Zola. Since his death, his fiction has been translated into almost a hundred languages, and has formed the basis for more than 200 motion pictures.

THE CENCI—1598

Should you ever go to Rome and visit the villa Pamphili, no doubt, after having sought under its tall pines and along its canals the shade and freshness so rare in the capital of the Christian world, you will descend towards the Janiculum Hill by a charming road, in the middle of which you will find the Pauline fountain. Having passed this monument, and having lingered a moment on the terrace of the church of St. Peter Montorio, which commands the whole of Rome, you will visit the cloister of Bramante, in the middle of which, sunk a few feet below the level, is built, on the identical place where St. Peter was crucified, a little temple, half Greek, half Christian; you will thence ascend by a side door into the church itself. There, the attentive cicerone will show you, in the first chapel to the right, the Christ Scourged, by Sebastian del Piombo, and in the third chapel to the left, an Entombment by Fiammingo; having examined these two masterpieces at leisure, he will take you to each end of the transverse cross, and will show you—on one side a picture by Salviati, on slate, and on the other a work by Vasari; then, pointing out in melancholy tones a copy of Guido's Martyrdom of St. Peter on the high altar, he will relate to you how for three centuries the divine Raffaelle's Transfiguration was worshipped in that spot; how it was carried away by the French in 1809, and restored to the pope by the Allies in 1814. As you have already in all probability admired this masterpiece in the Vatican, allow him to expatiate, and search at the foot of the altar for a mortuary slab, which you will identify by a cross and the single word; Orate; under this gravestone is buried Beatrice Cenci, whose tragical story cannot but impress you profoundly.

She was the daughter of Francesco Cenci. Whether or not it be true that men are born in harmony with their epoch, and that some embody its good qualities and others its bad ones, it may nevertheless interest our readers to cast a rapid glance over the period which had just passed when the events which we are about to relate took place. Francesco Cenci will then appear to them as the diabolical incarnation of his time.

On the 11th of August, 1492, after the lingering death-agony of Innocent VIII, during which two hundred and twenty murders were committed in the streets of Rome, Alexander VI ascended the pontifical throne. Son of a sister of Pope Calixtus III, Roderigo Lenzuoli Borgia, before being created cardinal, had five children by Rosa Vanozza, whom he afterwards caused to be married to a rich Roman. These children were:

Francis, Duke of Gandia;

Caesar, bishop and cardinal, afterwards Duke of Valentinois;

Lucrezia, who was married four times: her first husband was Giovanni Sforza, lord of Pesaro, whom she left owing to his impotence; the second, Alfonso, Duke of Bisiglia, whom her brother Caesar caused to be assassinated; the third, Alfonso d'Este, Duke of Ferrara, from whom a second divorce separated her; finally, the fourth, Alfonso of Aragon, who was stabbed to death on the steps of the basilica of St. Peter, and afterwards, three weeks later, strangled, because he did not die soon enough from his wounds, which nevertheless were mortal;

Giofre, Count of Squillace, of whom little is known;

And, finally, a youngest son, of whom nothing at all is known.

The most famous of these three brothers was Caesar Borgia. He had made every arrangement a plotter could make to be King of Italy at the death of his father the pope, and his measures were so carefully taken as to leave no doubt in his own mind as to the success of this vast project. Every chance was provided against, except one; but Satan himself could hardly have foreseen this particular one. The reader will judge for himself.

The pope had invited Cardinal Adrien to supper in his vineyard on the Belvidere; Cardinal Adrien was very rich, and the pope wished to inherit his wealth, as he already had acquired that of the Cardinals of Sant' Angelo, Capua, and Modena. To effect this, Caesar Borgia sent two bottles of poisoned wine to his father's cup-bearer, without taking him into his confidence; he only instructed him not to serve this wine till he himself gave orders to do so; unfortunately, during supper the cup-bearer left his post for a moment, and in this interval a careless butler served the poisoned wine to the pope, to Caesar Borgia, and to Cardinal Corneto.

Alexander VI died some hours afterwards; Caesar Borgia was confined to bed, and sloughed off his skin; while Cardinal

Corneto lost his sight and his senses, and was brought to death's door.

Pius III succeeded Alexander VI, and reigned twenty-five days; on the twenty-sixth he was poisoned also.

Caesar Borgia had under his control eighteen Spanish cardinals who owed to him their places in the Sacred College; these cardinals were entirely his creatures, and he could command them absolutely. As he was in a moribund condition and could make no use of them for himself, he sold them to Giuliano della Rovere, and Giuliano della Rovere was elected pope, under the name of Julius II. To the Rome of Nero succeeded the Athens of Pericles.

Leo X succeeded Julius II, and under his pontificate Christianity assumed a pagan character, which, passing from art into manners, gives to this epoch a strange complexion. Crimes for the moment disappeared, to give place to vices; but to charming vices, vices in good taste, such as those indulged in by Alcibiades and sung by Catullus. Leo X died after having assembled under his reign, which lasted eight years, eight months, and nineteen days, Michael Angelo, Raffaelle, Leonardo da Vinci, Correggio, Titian, Andrea del Sarto, Fra Bartolommeo, Giulio Romano, Ariosto, Guicciardini, and Macchiavelli.

Giulio di Medici and Pompeo Colonna had equal claims to succeed him. As both were skilful politicians, experienced courtiers, and moreover of real and almost equal merit, neither of them could obtain a majority, and the Conclave was prolonged almost indefinitely, to the great fatigue of the cardinals. So it happened one day that a cardinal, more tired than the rest, proposed to elect, instead of either Medici or Colonna, the son, some say of a weaver, others of a brewer of Utrecht, of whom no one had ever thought till then, and who was for the moment acting head of affairs in Spain, in the absence of Charles the Fifth. The jest prospered in the ears of those who heard it; all the cardinals approved their colleague's proposal, and Adrien became pope by a mere accident.

He was a perfect specimen of the Flemish type a regular Dutchman, and could not speak a word of Italian. When he arrived in Rome, and saw the Greek masterpieces of sculpture collected at vast cost by Leo X, he wished to break them to pieces, exclaiming, "Suet idola anticorum." His first act was to despatch a papal nuncio, Francesco Cherigato, to the Diet of Nuremberg, convened to discuss the reforms of Luther, with instructions which give a vivid notion of the manners of the time.

"Candidly confess," said he, "that God has permitted this schism and this persecution on account of the sins of man, and especially those of priests and prelates of the Church; for we know that many abominable things have taken place in the Holy See."

Adrien wished to bring the Romans back to the simple and austere manners of the early Church, and with this object pushed reform to the minutest details. For instance, of the hundred grooms maintained by Leo X, he retained only a dozen, in order, he said, to have two more than the cardinals.

A pope like this could not reign long: he died after a year's pontificate. The morning after his death his physician's door was found decorated with garlands of flowers, bearing this inscription: "To the liberator of his country."

Giulio di Medici and Pompeo Colonna were again rival candidates. Intrigues recommenced, and the Conclave was once more so divided that at one time the cardinals thought they could only escape the difficulty in which they were placed by doing what they had done before, and electing a third competitor; they were even talking about Cardinal Orsini, when Giulio di Medici, one of the rival candidates, hit upon a very ingenious expedient. He wanted only five votes; five of his partisans each offered to bet five of Colonna's a hundred thousand ducats to ten thousand against the election of Giulio di Medici. At the very first ballot after the wager, Giulio di Medici got the five votes he wanted; no objection could be made, the cardinals had not been bribed; they had made a bet, that was all.

Thus it happened, on the 18th of November, 1523, Giulio di Medici was proclaimed pope under the name of Clement VII. The same day, he generously paid the five hundred thousand ducats which his five partisans had lost.

It was under this pontificate, and during the seven months in which Rome, conquered by the Lutheran soldiers of the Constable of Bourbon, saw holy things subjected to the most frightful profanations, that Francesco Cenci was born.

He was the son of Monsignor Nicolo Cenci, afterwards apostolic treasurer during the pontificate of Pius V. Under this venerable prelate, who occupied himself much more with the spiritual than the temporal administration of his kingdom, Nicolo Cenci took advantage of his spiritual head's abstraction of worldly matters to amass a net revenue of a hundred and sixty thousand piastres, about f32,000 of our money. Francesco Cenci, who was his only son, inherited this fortune.

His youth was spent under popes so occupied with the schism of Luther that they had no time to think of anything else. The result was, that Francesco Cenci, inheriting vicious instincts and master of an immense fortune which enabled him to purchase immunity, abandoned himself to all the evil passions of his fiery and passionate temperament. Five times during his profligate career imprisoned for abominable crimes, he only succeeded in procuring his liberation by the payment of two hundred thousand piastres, or about one million francs. It should be explained that popes at this time were in great need of money.

The lawless profligacy of Francesco Cenci first began seriously to attract public attention under the pontificate of Gregory XIII. This reign offered marvellous facilities for the development of a reputation such as that which this reckless Italian Don Juan seemed bent on acquiring. Under the Bolognese Buoncampagno, a free hand was given to those able to pay both assassins and judges. Rape and murder were so common that public justice scarcely troubled itself with these trifling things, if nobody appeared to prosecute the guilty parties. The good Gregory had his reward for his easygoing indulgence; he was spared to rejoice over the Massacre of St. Bartholomew.

Francesco Cenci was at the time of which we are speaking a man of forty-four or forty-five years of age, about five feet four inches in height, symmetrically proportioned, and very strong, although rather thin; his hair was streaked with grey, his eyes were large and expressive, although the upper eyelids drooped somewhat; his nose was long, his lips were thin, and wore habitually a pleasant smile, except when his eye perceived an enemy; at this moment his features assumed a terrible expression; on such occasions, and whenever moved or even slightly irritated, he was seized with a fit of nervous trembling, which lasted long after the cause which provoked it had passed. An adept in all manly exercises and especially in horsemanship, he sometimes used to ride without stopping from Rome to Naples, a distance of forty-one leagues, passing through the forest of San Germano and the Pontine marshes heedless of brigands, although he might be alone and unarmed save for his sword and dagger. When his horse fell from fatigue, he bought another; were the owner unwilling to sell he took it by force; if resistance were made, he struck, and always with the point, never the hilt. In most cases, being well known throughout the Papal States as a free-handed person, nobody tried to thwart him; some yielding through fear, others from motives of interest. Impious, sacrilegious, and atheistical, he never entered a church except to profane its sanctity. It was said of him that he had a morbid appetite for novelties in crime, and that there was no outrage he would not commit if he hoped by so doing to enjoy a new sensation.

At the age of about forty-five he had married a very rich woman, whose name is not mentioned by any chronicler. She died, leaving him seven children—five boys and two girls. He then married Lucrezia Petroni, a perfect beauty of the Roman type, except for the ivory pallor of her complexion. By this second marriage he had no children.

As if Francesco Cenci were void of all natural affection, he hated his children, and was at no pains to conceal his feelings towards them: on one occasion, when he was building, in the courtyard of his magnificent palace, near the Tiber, a chapel dedicated to St. Thomas, he remarked to the architect, when instructing him to design a family vault, "That is where I hope to bury them all." The architect often subsequently admitted that he was so terrified by the fiendish laugh which accompanied these words, that had not Francesco Cenci's work been extremely profitable, he would have refused to go on with it.

As soon as his three eldest boys, Giacomo, Cristoforo, and Rocco, were out of their tutors' hands, in order to get rid of them he sent them to the University of Salamanca, where, out of sight, they were out of mind, for he thought no more about them, and did not even send them the means of subsistence. In these straits, after struggling for some months against their wretched plight, the lads were obliged to leave Salamanca, and beg their way home, tramping barefoot through France and Italy, till they made their way back to Rome, where they found their father harsher and more unkind than ever.

This happened in the early part of the reign of Clement VIII, famed for his justice. The three youths resolved to apply to him, to grant them an allowance out of their father's immense income. They consequently repaired to Frascati, where the pope was building the beautiful Aldobrandini Villa, and stated their case. The pope admitted the justice of their claims, and ordered Francesco, to allow each of them two thousand crowns a year. He endeavoured by every possible means to evade this decree, but the pope's orders were too stringent to be disobeyed.

About this period he was for the third time imprisoned for infamous crimes. His three sons them again petitioned the pope, alleging that their father dishonoured the family name, and praying that the extreme rigour of the law, a capital sentence, should be enforced in his case. The pope pronounced this conduct unnatural and odious, and drove them with ignominy from his presence. As for Francesco, he escaped, as on the two previous occasions, by the payment of a large sum of money.

It will be readily understood that his sons' conduct on this occasion did not improve their father's disposition towards them, but as their independent pensions enabled them to keep out of his way, his rage fell with all the greater intensity on his two unhappy daughters. Their situation soon became so intolerable, that the elder, contriving to elude the close supervision under which she was kept, forwarded to the pope a petition, relating the cruel treatment to which she was subjected, and praying His Holiness either to give her in marriage or place her in a convent. Clement VIII took pity on her; compelled Francesco Cenci to give her a dowry of sixty thousand crowns, and married her to Carlo Gabrielli, of a noble family of Gubbio. Francesco driven nearly frantic with rage when he saw this victim released from his clutches.

About the same time death relieved him from two other encumbrances: his sons Rocco and Cristoforo were killed within a year of each other; the latter by a bungling medical practitioner whose name is unknown; the former by Paolo Corso di Massa, in the streets of Rome. This came as a relief to Francesco, whose avarice pursued his sons even after their death, far he intimated to the priest that he would not spend a farthing on funeral services. They were accordingly borne to the paupers' graves which he had caused to be prepared for them, and when he saw them both interred, he cried out that he was well rid of such good-for-nothing children, but that he should be perfectly happy only when the remaining five were buried with the first two, and that when he had got rid of the last he himself would burn down his palace as a bonfire to celebrate the event.

But Francesco took every precaution against his second daughter, Beatrice Cenci, following the example of her elder sister. She was then a child of twelve or thirteen years of age, beautiful and innocent as an angel. Her long fair hair, a beauty seen so rarely in Italy, that Raffaelle, believing it divine, has appropriated it to all his Madonnas, curtained a lovely forehead, and fell in flowing locks over her shoulders. Her azure eyes bore a heavenly expression; she was of middle height, exquisitely proportioned; and during the rare moments when a gleam of happiness allowed her natural character to display itself, she was lively, joyous, and sympathetic, but at the same time evinced a firm and decided disposition.

To make sure of her custody, Francesco kept her shut up in a remote apartment of his palace, the key of which he kept in his own possession. There, her unnatural and inflexible gaoler daily brought her some food. Up to the age of thirteen, which she had now reached, he had behaved to her with the most extreme harshness and severity; but now, to poor Beatrice's great astonishment, he all at once became gentle and even tender. Beatrice was a child no longer; her beauty expanded like a flower; and Francesco, a stranger to no crime, however heinous, had marked her for his own.

Brought up as she had been, uneducated, deprived of all society, even that of her stepmother, Beatrice knew not good from evil: her ruin was comparatively easy to compass; yet Francesco, to accomplish his diabolical purpose, employed all the means at his command. Every night she was awakened by a concert of music which seemed to come from Paradise. When she mentioned this to her father, he left her in this belief, adding that if she proved gentle and obedient she would be rewarded by heavenly sights, as well as heavenly sounds.

One night it came to pass that as the young girl was reposing, her head supported on her elbow, and listening to a delightful harmony, the chamber door suddenly opened, and from the darkness of her own room she beheld a suite of apartments brilliantly illuminated, and sensuous with perfumes; beautiful youths and girls, half clad, such as she had seen in the pictures of Guido and Raffaelle, moved to and fro in these apartments, seeming full of joy and happiness: these were the ministers to the pleasures of Francesco, who, rich as a king, every night revelled in the orgies of Alexander, the wedding revels of Lucrezia, and the excesses of Tiberius at Capri. After an hour, the door closed, and the seductive vision vanished, leaving Beatrice full of trouble and amazement.

The night following, the same apparition again presented itself, only, on this occasion, Francesco Cenci, undressed, entered his daughter's roam and invited her to join the fete. Hardly knowing what she did, Beatrice yet perceived the impropriety of yielding to her father's wishes: she replied that, not seeing her stepmother, Lucrezia Petroni, among all these women, she dared not leave her bed to mix with persons who were unknown to her. Francesco threatened and prayed, but threats and prayers were of no avail. Beatrice wrapped herself up in the bedclothes, and obstinately refused to obey.

The next night she threw herself on her bed without undressing. At the accustomed hour the door opened, and the nocturnal spectacle reappeared. This time, Lucrezia Petroni was among the women who passed before Beatrice's door; violence had compelled her to undergo this humiliation. Beatrice was too far off to see her blushes and her tears. Francesco pointed out her stepmother, whom she had lacked for in vain the previous evening; and as she could no longer make any opposition, he led her, covered with blushes and confusion, into the middle of this orgy.

Beatrice there saw incredible and infamous things....

Nevertheless, she resisted a long time: an inward voice told her that this was horrible; but Francesco had the slaw persistence of a demon. To these sights, calculated to stimulate her passions, he added heresies designed to warp her mind; he told her that the greatest saints venerated by the Church were the issue of fathers and daughters, and in the end Beatrice committed a crime without even knowing it to be a sin.

His brutality then knew no bounds. He forced Lucrezia and Beatrice to share the same bed, threatening his wife to kill her if she disclosed to his daughter by a single word that there was anything odious in such an intercourse. So matters went on for about three years.

At this time Francesco was obliged to make a journey, and leave the women alone and free. The first thing Lucrezia did was to enlighten Beatrice an the infamy of the life they were leading; they then together prepared a memorial to the pope, in which they laid before him a statement of all the blows and outrages they had suffered. But, before leaving, Francesco Cenci had taken precautions; every person about the pope was in his pay, or hoped to be. The petition never reached His Holiness, and the two poor women, remembering that Clement VIII had on a farmer occasion driven Giacomo, Cristaforo, and Rocco from his presence, thought they were included in the same proscription, and looked upon themselves as abandoned to their fate.

When matters were in this state, Giacomo, taking advantage of his father's absence, came to pay them a visit with a friend of his, an abbe named Guerra: he was a young man of twenty-five or twenty-six, belonging to one of the most noble families in Rome, of a bold, resolute, and courageous character, and idolised by all the Roman ladies for his beauty. To classical features he added blue eyes swimming in poetic sentiment; his hair was long and fair, with chestnut beard and eyebrows; add to these attractions a highly educated mind, natural eloquence expressed by a musical and penetrating voice, and the reader may form some idea of Monsignor the Abbe Guerra.

No sooner had he seen Beatrice than he fell in love with her. On her side, she was not slow to return the sympathy of the young priest. The Council of Trent had not been held at that time, consequently ecclesiastics were not precluded from marriage. It was therefore decided that on the return of Francesco the Abbe Guerra should demand the hand of Beatrice from her father, and the women, happy in the absence of their master, continued to live on, hoping for better things to come.

After three or four months, during which no one knew where he was, Francesco returned. The very first night, he wished to resume his intercourse with Beatrice; but she was no longer the same person, the timid and submissive child had become a girl of decided will; strong in her love for the abbe, she resisted alike prayers, threats, and blows.

The wrath of Francesco fell upon his wife, whom he accused of betraying him; he gave her a violent thrashing. Lucrezia Petroni was a veritable Roman she-wolf, passionate alike in love and vengeance; she endured all, but pardoned nothing.

Some days after this, the Abbe Guerra arrived at the Cenci palace to carry out what had been arranged. Rich, young, noble, and handsome, everything would seem to promise him success; yet he was rudely dismissed by Francesco. The first refusal did not daunt him; he returned to the charge a second time and yet a third, insisting upon the suitableness of such a union. At length Francesco, losing patience, told this obstinate lover that a reason existed why Beatrice could be neither his wife nor any other man's. Guerra demanded what this reason was. Francesco replied:

"Because she is my mistress."

Monsignor Guerra turned pale at this answer, although at first he did not believe a word of it; but when he saw the smile with which Francesco Cenci accompanied his words, he was compelled to believe that, terrible though it was, the truth had been spoken.

For three days he sought an interview with Beatrice in vain; at length he succeeded in finding her. His last hope was her denial of this horrible story: Beatrice confessed all. Henceforth there was no human hope for the two lovers; an impassable gulf separated them. They parted bathed in tears, promising to love one another always.

Up to that time the two women had not formed any criminal resolution, and possibly the tragical incident might never have happened, had not Frances one night returned into his daughter's room and violently forced her into the commission of fresh crime.

Henceforth the doom of Francesco was irrevocably pronounced.

As we have said, the mind of Beatrice was susceptible to the best and the worst influences: it could attain excellence, and descend to guilt. She went and told her mother of the fresh outrage she had undergone; this roused in the heart of the other woman the sting of her own wrongs; and, stimulating each other's desire for revenge, they, decided upon the murder of Francesco.

Guerra was called in to this council of death. His heart was a prey to hatred and revenge. He undertook to communicate with Giacomo Cenci, without whose concurrence the women would not act, as he was the head of the family, when his father was left out of account.

Giacomo entered readily into the conspiracy. It will be remembered what he had formerly suffered from his father; since that time he had married, and the close-fisted old man had left him, with his wife and children, to languish in poverty. Guerra's house was selected to meet in and concert matters.

Giacomo hired a sbirro named Marzio, and Guerra a second named Olympio.

Both these men had private reasons for committing

the crime—one being actuated by love, the other by hatred. Marzio, who was in the service of Giacomo, had often seen Beatrice, and loved her, but with that silent and hopeless love which devours the soul. When he conceived that the proposed crime would draw him nearer to Beatrice, he accepted his part in it without any demur.

As for Olympio, he hated Francesco, because the latter had caused him to lose the post of castellan of Rocco Petrella, a fortified stronghold in the kingdom of Naples, belonging to Prince Colonna. Almost every year Francesco Cenci spent some months at Rocco Petrella with his family; for Prince Colonna, a noble and magnificent but needy prince, had much esteem for Francesco, whose purse he found extremely useful. It had so happened that Francesco, being dissatisfied with Olympio, complained about him to Prince Colonna, and he was dismissed.

After several consultations between the Cenci family, the abbe and the sbirri, the following plan of action was decided upon.

The period when Francesco Cenci was accustomed to go to Rocco Petrella was approaching: it was arranged that Olympio, conversant with the district and its inhabitants, should collect a party of a dozen Neapolitan bandits, and conceal them in a forest through which the travellers would have to pass. Upon a given signal, the whole family were to be seized and carried off. A heavy ransom was to be demanded, and the sons were to be sent back to Rome to raise the sum; but, under pretext of inability to do so, they were to allow the time fixed by the bandits to lapse, when Francesco was to be put to death. Thus all suspicions of a plot would be avoided, and the real assassins would escape justice.

This well-devised scheme was nevertheless unsuccessful. When Francesco left Rome, the scout sent in advance by the conspirators could not find the bandits; the latter, not being warned beforehand, failed to come down before the passage of the travellers, who arrived safe and sound at Rocco Petreila. The bandits, after having patrolled the road in vain, came to the conclusion that their prey had escaped, and, unwilling to stay any longer in a place where they had already spent a week, went off in quest of better luck elsewhere.

Francesco had in the meantime settled down in the fortress, and, to be more free to tyrannise over Lucrezia and Beatrice, sent back to Rome Giacomo and his two other sons. He then recommenced his infamous attempts upon Beatrice, and with such persistence, that she resolved herself to accomplish the deed which at first she desired to entrust to other hands.

Olympio and Marzio, who had nothing to fear from justice, remained lurking about the castle; one day Beatrice saw them from a window, and made signs that she had something to communicate to them. The same night Olympio, who having been castellan knew all the approaches to the fortress, made his way there with his companion. Beatrice awaited them at a window which looked on to a secluded courtyard; she gave them letters which she had written to her brother and to Monsignor Guerra. The former was to approve, as he had done before, the murder of their father; for she would do nothing without his sanction. As for Monsignor Guerra, he was to pay Olympio a thousand piastres, half the stipulated sum; Marzio acting out of pure love for Beatrice, whom he worshipped as a Madonna; which observing, the girl gave him a handsome scarlet mantle, trimmed with gold lace, telling him to wear it for love of her. As for the remaining moiety, it was to be paid when the death of the old man had placed his wife and daughter in possession of his fortune.

The two sbirri departed, and the imprisoned conspirators anxiously awaited their return. On the day fixed, they were seen again. Monsignor Guerra had paid the thousand piastres, and Giacomo had given his consent. Nothing now stood in the way of the execution of this terrible deed, which was fixed for the 8th of September, the day of the Nativity of the Virgin; but Signora Lucrezia, a very devout person, having noticed this circumstance, would not be a party to the committal of a double sin; the matter was therefore deferred till the next day, the 9th.

That evening, the 9th of September, 1598, the two women, supping with the old man, mixed some narcotic with his wine so adroitly that, suspicious though he was, he never detected it, and having swallowed the potion, soon fell into a deep sleep.

The evening previous, Marzio and Olympio had been admitted into the castle, where they had lain concealed all night and all day; for, as will be remembered, the assassination would have been effected the day before had it not been for the religious scruples of Signora Lucrezia Petroni. Towards midnight, Beatrice fetched them out of their hiding-place, and took them to her father's chamber, the door of which she herself opened. The assassins entered, and the two women awaited the issue in the room adjoining.

After a moment, seeing the sbirri reappear pale and nerveless, shaking their heads without speaking, they at once inferred that nothing had been done.

"What is the matter?" cried Beatrice; "and what hinders you?"

"It is a cowardly act," replied the assassins, "to kill a poor old man in his sleep. At the thought of his age, we were struck with pity."

Then Beatrice disdainfully raised her head, and in a deep firm voice thus reproached them.

"Is it possible that you, who pretend to be brave and strong, have not courage enough to kill a sleeping old man? How would it be if he were awake? And thus you steal our money! Very well: since your cowardice compels me to do so, I will kill my father myself; but you will not long survive him."

Hearing these words, the sbirri felt ashamed of their irresolution, and, indicating by signs that they would fulfil their compact, they entered the room, accompanied by the two women. As they had said, a ray of moonlight shone through the open window, and brought into prominence the tranquil face of the old man, the sight of whose white hair had so affected them.

This time they showed no mercy. One of them carried two great nails, such as those portrayed in pictures of the Crucifixion; the other bore a mallet: the first placed a nail upright over one of the old man's eyes; the other struck it with the hammer, and drove it into his head. The throat was pierced in the same way with the second nail; and thus the guilty soul, stained throughout its career with crimes of violence, was in its turn violently torn from the body, which lay writhing on the floor where it had rolled.

The young girl then, faithful to her word, handed the sbirri a large purse containing the rest of the sum agreed upon, and they left. When they found themselves alone, the women drew the nails out of the wounds, wrapped the corpse in a sheet, and dragged it through the rooms towards a small rampart, intending to throw it down into a garden which had been allowed to run to waste. They hoped that the old man's death would be attributed to his having accidentally fallen off the terrace on his way in the dark to a closet at the end of the gallery. But their strength failed them when they reached the door of the last room, and, while resting there, Lucrezia perceived the two sbirri, sharing the money before making their escape. At her call they came to her, carried the corpse to the rampart, and, from a spot pointed out by the women, where the terrace was unfenced by any parapet, they threw it into an elder tree below, whose branches retained'it suspended.

When the body was found the following morning hanging in the branches of the elder tree, everybody supposed, as Beatrice and her stepmother had foreseen, that Francesco, stepping over the edge of the 386 terrace in the dark, had thus met his end. The body was so scratched and disfigured that no one noticed the wounds made by the two nails. The ladies, as soon as the news was imparted to them, came out from their rooms, weeping and lamenting in so natural a manner as to disarm any suspicions. The only person who formed any was the laundress to whom Beatrice entrusted the sheet in which her father's body had been wrapped, accounting for its bloody condition by a lame explanation, which the laundress accepted without question, or pretended to do so; and immediately after the funeral, the mourners returned to Rome, hoping at length to enjoy quietude and peace. For some time, indeed, they did enjoy tranquillity, perhaps poisoned by remorse, but ere long retribution pursued them. The court of Naples, hearing of the sudden and unexpected death of Francesco Cenci, and conceiving some suspicions of violence, despatched a royal commissioner to Petrella to exhume the body and make minute inquiries, if there appeared to be adequate grounds for doing so. On his arrival all the domestics in the castle were placed under arrest and sent in chains to Naples. No incriminating proofs, however, were found, except in the evidence of the laundress, who deposed that Beatrice had given her a bloodstained sheet to wash. This, clue led to terrible consequences; for, further questioned she declared that she could not believe the explanation given to account for its condition. The evidence was sent to the Roman court; but at that period it did not appear strong enough to warrant the arrest of the Cenci family, who remained undisturbed for many months, during which time the youngest boy died. Of the five brothers there only remained Giacomo, the eldest, and Bernardo, the youngest but one. Nothing prevented them from escaping to Venice or Florence; but they remained quietly in Rome.

Meantime Monsignor Guerra received private information that, shortly before the death of Francesco, Marzio and Olympio had been seen prowling round the castle, and that the Neapolitan police had received orders to arrest them.

The monsignor was a most wary man, and very difficult to catch napping when warned in time. He immediately hired two other sbirri to assassinate Marzio and Olympio. The one commissioned to put Olympio out of the way came across him at Terni, and conscientiously did his work with a poniard, but Marzio's man unfortunately arrived at Naples too late, and found his bird already in the hands of the police.

He was put to the torture, and confessed everything. His deposition was sent to Rome, whither he shortly afterwards followed it, to be confronted with the accused. Warrants were immediately issued for the arrest of Giacomo, Bernardo, Lucrezia, and Beatrice; they were at first confined in the Cenci palace under a strong guard, but the proofs against them becoming stronger and stronger, they were removed to the castle of Corte Savella, where they were confronted with Marzio; but they obstinately denied both any complicity in the crime and any knowledge of the assassin. Beatrice, above all, displayed the greatest assurance, demanding to be the first to be confronted with Marzio; whose mendacity she affirmed with such calm dignity, that he, more than ever smitten by her beauty, determined, since he could not live for her, to save her by his death. Consequently, he declared all his statements to be false, and asked forgiveness from God and from Beatrice; neither threats nor tortures could make him recant, and he died firm in his denial, under frightful tortures. The Cenci then thought themselves safe.

God's justice, however, still pursued them. The sbirro who had killed Olympio happened to be arrested for another crime, and, making a clean breast, confessed that he had been employed by Monsignor Guerra—to put out of the way a fellow-assassin named Olympio, who knew too many of the monsignor's secrets.

Luckily for himself, Monsignor Guerra heard of this opportunely. A man of infinite resource, he lost not a moment in timid or irresolute plans, but as it happened that at the very moment when he was warned, the charcoal dealer who supplied his house with fuel was at hand, he sent for him, purchased his silence with a handsome bribe, and then, buying for almost their weight in gold the dirty old clothes which he wore, he assumed these, cut off all his beautiful cherished fair hair, stained his beard, smudged his face, bought two asses, laden with charcoal, and limped up and down the streets of Rome, crying, "Charcoal! charcoal!" Then, whilst all the detectives were hunting high and low for him, he got out of the city, met a company of merchants under escort, joined them, and reached Naples, where he embarked. What ultimately became of him was never known; it has been asserted, but without confirmation, that he succeeded—in reaching France, and enlisted in a Swiss regiment in the pay of Henry IV.

The confession of the sbirro and the disappearance of Monsignor Guerra left no moral doubt of the guilt of the Cenci. They were consequently sent from the castle to the prison; the two brothers, when put to the torture, broke down and confessed their guilt. Lucrezia Petroni's full habit of body rendered her unable to bear the torture of the rope, and, on being suspended in the air, begged to be lowered, when she confessed all she knew.

As for Beatrice, she continued unmoved; neither promises, threats, nor torture had any effect upon her; she bore everything unflinchingly, and the judge Ulysses Moscati himself, famous though he was in such matters, failed to draw from her a single incriminating word. Unwilling to take any further responsibility, he referred the case to Clement VIII; and the pope, conjecturing that the judge had been too lenient in applying the torture to, a young and beautiful Roman lady, took it out of his hands and entrusted it to another judge, whose severity and insensibility to emotion were undisputed.

This latter reopened the whole interrogatory, and as Beatrice up to that time had only been subjected to the ordinary torture, he gave instructions to apply both the ordinary and extraordinary. This was the rope and pulley, one of the most terrible inventions ever devised by the most ingenious of tormentors.

To make the nature of this horrid torture plain to our readers, we give a detailed description of it, adding an extract of the presiding judge's report of the case, taken from the Vatican manuscripts.

Of the various forms of torture then used in Rome the most common were the whistle, the fire, the sleepless, and the rope.

The mildest, the torture of the whistle, was used only in the case of children and old persons; it consisted in thrusting between the nails and the flesh reeds cut in the shape of whistles.

The fire, frequently employed before the invention of the sleepless torture, was simply roasting the soles of the feet before a hot fire.

The sleepless torture, invented by Marsilius, was worked by forcing the accused into an angular frame of wood about five feet high, the sufferer being stripped and his arms tied behind his back to the frame; two men, relieved every five hours, sat beside him, and roused him the moment he closed his eyes. Marsilius says he has never found a man proof against this torture; but here he claims more than he is justly entitled to. Farinacci states that, out of one hundred accused persons subjected to it, five only refused to confess—a very satisfactory result for the inventor.

Lastly comes the torture of the rope and pulley, the most in vogue of all, and known in other Latin countries as the strappado.

It was divided into three degrees of intensity—the slight, the severe, and the very severe.

The first, or slight torture, which consisted mainly in the apprehensions it caused, comprised the threat of severe torture, introduction into the torture chamber, stripping, and the tying of the rope in readiness for its appliance. To increase the terror these preliminaries excited, a pang of physical pain was added by tightening a cord round the wrists. This often sufficed to extract a confession from women or men of highly strung nerves.

The second degree, or severe torture, consisted in fastening the sufferer, stripped naked, and his hands tied behind his back, by the wrists to one end of a rope passed round a pulley bolted into the vaulted ceiling, the other end being attached to a windlass, by turning which he could be hoisted, into the air, and dropped again, either slowly or with a jerk, as ordered by the judge. The suspension generally lasted during the recital of a Pater Noster, an Ave Maria, or a Miserere; if the accused persisted in his denial, it was doubled. This second degree, the last of the ordinary torture, was put in practice when the crime appeared reasonably probable but was not absolutely proved.

The third, or very severe, the first of the extraordinary forms of torture, was so called when the sufferer, having hung suspended by the wrists, for sometimes a whole hour, was swung about by the executioner, either like the pendulum of a clock, or by elevating him with the windlass and dropping him to within a foot or two of the ground. If he stood this torture, a thing almost unheard of, seeing that it cut the flesh of the wrist to the bone and dislocated the limbs, weights were attached to the feet, thus doubling the torture. This last form of torture was only applied when an atrocious crime had been proved to have been committed upon a sacred person, such as a priest, a cardinal, a prince, or an eminent and learned man.

Having seen that Beatrice was sentenced to the torture ordinary and extraordinary, and having explained the nature of these tortures, we proceed to quote the official report:—

"And as in reply to every question she would confess nothing, we caused her to be taken by two officers and led from the prison to the torture chamber, where the torturer was in attendance; there, after cutting off her hair, he made her sit on a small stool, undressed her, pulled off her shoes, tied her hands behind her back, fastened them to a rope passed over a pulley bolted into the ceiling of the aforesaid chamber, and wound up at the other end by a four lever windlass, worked by two men."

"Before hoisting her from the ground we again interrogated her touching the aforesaid parricide; but notwithstanding the confessions of her brother and her stepmother, which were again produced, bearing their signatures, she persisted in denying everything, saying, 'Haul me about and do what you like with me; I have spoken the truth, and will tell you nothing else, even if I were torn to pieces.'

"Upon this we had her hoisted in the air by the wrists

to the height of about two feet from the ground, while we recited a Pater Noster; and then again questioned her as to the facts and circumstances of the aforesaid parricide; but she would make no further answer, only saying, 'You are killing me! You are killing me!'

"We then raised her to the elevation of four feet, and began an Ave Maria. But before our prayer was half finished she fainted away; or pretended to do so.

"We caused a bucketful of water to be thrown over her head; feeling its coolness, she recovered consciousness, and cried, 'My God! I am dead! You are killing me! My God!' But this was all she would say.

"We then raised her higher still, and recited a Miserere, during which, instead of joining in the prayer, she shook convulsively and cried several times, 'My God! My God!'

"Again questioned as to the aforesaid parricide, she would confess nothing, saying only that she was innocent, and then again fainted away.

"We caused more water to be thrown over her; then she recovered her senses, opened her eyes, and cried, 'O cursed executioners! You are killing me! You are killing me!' But nothing more would she say.

"Seeing which, and that she persisted in her denial, we ordered the torturer to proceed to the torture by jerks.

"He accordingly hoisted her ten feet from the ground, and when there we enjoined her to tell the truth; but whether she would not or could not speak, she answered only by a motion of the head indicating that she could say nothing.

"Seeing which, we made a sign to the executioner, to let go the rope, and she fell with all her weight from the height of ten feet to that of two feet; her arms, from the shock, were dislocated from their sockets; she uttered a loud cry, and swooned away.

"We again caused water to be dashed in her face; she returned to herself, and again cried out, 'Infamous assassins! You are killing me; but were you to tear out my arms, I would tell you nothing else.'

"Upon this, we ordered a weight of fifty pounds to be fastened to her feet. But at this moment the door opened, and many voices cried, 'Enough! Enough! Do not torture her any more!'"

These voices were those of Giacomo, Bernardo, and Lucrezia Petroni. The judges, perceiving the obstinacy of Beatrice, had ordered that the accused, who had been separated for five months, should be confronted.

They advanced into the torture chamber, and seeing Beatrice hanging by the wrists, her arms disjointed, and covered with blood, Giacomo cried out:—

"The sin is committed; nothing further remains but to save our souls by repentance, undergo death courageously, and not suffer you to be thus tortured."

Then said Beatrice, shaking her head as if to cast off grief—

"Do you then wish to die? Since you wish it, be it so."

Then turning to the officers:—

"Untie me," said she, "read the examination to me; and

what I have to confess, I will confess; what I have to deny, I will deny."

Beatrice was then lowered and untied; a barber reduced the dislocation of her arms in the usual manner; the examination was read over to her, and, as she had promised, she made a full confession.

After this confession, at the request of the two brothers, they were all confined in the same prison; but the next day Giacomo and Bernardo were taken to the cells of Tordinona; as for the women, they remained where they were.

The pope was so horrified on reading the particulars of the crime contained in the confessions, that he ordered the culprits to be dragged by wild horses through the streets of Rome. But so barbarous a sentence shocked the public mind, so much so that many persons of princely rank petitioned the Holy Father on their knees, imploring him to reconsider his decree, or at least allow the accused to be heard in their defence.

"Tell me," replied Clement VIII, "did they give their unhappy father time to be heard in his own defence, when they slew him in so merciless and degrading a fashion?"

At length, overcome by so many entreaties, he respited them for three days.

The most eloquent and skilful advocates in Rome immediately busied themselves in preparing pleadings for so emotional a case, and on the day fixed for hearing appeared before His Holiness.

The first pleader was Nicolo degli Angeli, who spoke

with such force and eloquence that the pope, alarmed at the effect he was producing among the audience, passionately interrupted him.

"Are there then to be found," he indignantly cried, "among the Roman nobility children capable of killing their parents, and among Roman lawyers men capable of speaking in their defence? This is a thing we should never have believed, nor even for a moment supposed it possible!"

All were silent upon this terrible rebuke, except Farinacci, who, nerving himself with a strong sense of duty, replied respectfully but firmly—

"Most Holy Father, we are not here to defend criminals, but to save the innocent; for if we succeeded in proving that any of the accused acted in self-defence, I hope that they will be exonerated in the eyes of your Holiness; for just as the law provides for cases in which the father may legally kill the child, so this holds good in the converse. We will therefore continue our pleadings on receiving leave from your Holiness to do so."

Clement VIII then showed himself as patient as he had previously been hasty, and heard the argument of Farinacci, who pleaded that Francesco Cenci had lost all the rights of a father from, the day that he violated his daughter. In support of his contention he wished to put in the memorial sent by Beatrice to His Holiness, petitioning him, as her sister had done, to remove her from the paternal roof and place her in a convent. Unfortunately, this petition had disappeared, and notwithstanding the minutest search among the papal documents, no trace of it could be found.

The pope had all the pleadings collected, and dismissed the advocates, who then retired, excepting d'Altieri, who knelt before him, saying—

"Most Holy Father, I humbly ask pardon for appearing before you in this case, but I had no choice in the matter, being the advocate of the poor."

The pope kindly raised him, saying:

"Go; we are not surprised at your conduct, but at that of others, who protect and defend criminals."

As the pope took a great interest in this case, he sat up all night over it, studying it with Cardinal di San Marcello, a man of much acumen and great experience in criminal cases. Then, having summed it up, he sent a draft of his opinion to the advocates, who read it with great satisfaction, and entertained hopes that the lives of the convicted persons would be spared; for the evidence all went to prove that even if the children had taken their father's life, all the provocation came from him, and that Beatrice in particular had been dragged into the part she had taken in this crime by the tyranny, wickedness, and brutality of her father. Under the influence of these considerations the pope mitigated the severity of their prison life, and even allowed the prisoners to hope that their lives would not be forfeited.

Amidst the general feeling of relief afforded to the public by these favours, another tragical event changed the papal mind and frustrated all his humane intentions. This was the atrocious murder of the Marchese di Santa Croce, a man seventy years of age, by his son Paolo, who stabbed him with a dagger in fifteen or twenty places, because the father would not promise to make Paolo his sole heir. The murderer fled and escaped.

Clement VIII was horror-stricken at the increasing frequency of this crime of parricide: for the moment, however, he was unable to take action, having to go to Monte Cavallo to consecrate a cardinal titular bishop in the church of Santa Maria degli Angeli; but the day following, on Friday the 10th of September 1599, at eight o'clock in the morning, he summoned Monsignor Taverna, governor of Rome, and said to him—

"Monsignor, we place in your hands the Cenci case, that you may carry out the sentence as speedily as possible."

On his return to his palace, after leaving His Holiness, the governor convened a meeting of all the criminal judges in the city, the result of the council being that all the Cenci were condemned to death.

The final sentence was immediately known; and as this unhappy family inspired a constantly increasing interest, many cardinals spent the whole of the night either on horseback or in their carriages, making interest that, at least so far as the women were concerned, they should be put to death privately and in the prison, and that a free pardon should be granted to Bernardo, a poor lad only fifteen years of age, who, guiltless of any participation in the crime, yet found himself involved in its consequences. The one who interested himself most in the case was Cardinal Sforza, who nevertheless failed to elicit a single gleam of hope, so obdurate was His Holiness. At length Farinacci, working on the papal conscience, succeeded, after long and urgent entreaties, and only at the last moment, that the life of Bernardo should be spared.

From Friday evening the members of the brotherhood of the Conforteria had gathered at the two prisons of Corte Savella and Tordinona. The preparations for the closing scene of the tragedy had occupied workmen on the bridge of Sant' Angelo all night; and it was not till five o'clock in the morning that the registrar entered the cell of Lucrezia and Beatrice to read their sentences to them.

Both were sleeping, calm in the belief of a reprieve. The registrar woke them, and told them that, judged by man, they must now prepare to appear before God.

Beatrice was at first thunderstruck: she seemed paralysed and speechless; then she rose from bed, and staggering as if intoxicated, recovered her speech, uttering despairing cries. Lucrezia heard the tidings with more firmness, and proceeded to dress herself to go to the chapel, exhorting Beatrice to resignation; but she, raving, wrung her, hands and struck her head against the wall, shrieking, "To die! to die! Am I to die unprepared, on a scaffold! on a gibbet! My God! my God!" This fit led to a terrible paroxysm, after which the exhaustion of her body enabled her mind to recover its balance, and from that moment she became an angel of humility and an example of resignation.

Her first request was for a notary to make her will.

This was immediately complied with, and on his arrival she dictated its provisions with much calmness and precision. Its last clause desired her interment in the church of San Pietro in Montorio, for which she always had a strong attachment, as it commanded a view of her father's palace. She bequeathed five hundred crowns to the nuns of the order of the Stigmata, and ordered that her dowry; amounting to fifteen thousand crowns, should be distributed in marriage portions to fifty poor girls. She selected the foot of the high altar as the place where she wished to be buried, over which hung the beautiful picture of the Transfiguration, so often admired by her during her life.

Following her example, Lucrezia in her turn, disposed of her property: she desired to be buried in the church of San Giorgio di Velobre, and left thirty-two thousand crowns to charities, with other pious legacies. Having settled their earthly affairs, they joined in prayer, reciting psalms, litanies, and prayers far the dying.

At eight o'clock they confessed, heard mass, and received the sacraments; after which Beatrice, observing to her stepmother that the rich dresses they wore were out of place on a scaffold, ordered two to be made in nun's fashion—that is to say, gathered at the neck, with long wide sleeves. That for Lucrezia was made of black cotton stuff, Beatrice's of taffetas. In addition she had a small black turban made to place on her head. These dresses, with cords for girdles, were brought them; they were placed on a chair, while the women continued to pray.

The time appointed being near at hand, they were informed that their last moment was approaching. Then Beatrice, who was still on her knees, rose with a tranquil and almost joyful countenance. "Mother," said she, "the moment of our suffering is impending; I think we had better dress in these clothes, and help one another at our toilet for the last time." They then put on the dresses provided, girt themselves with the cords; Beatrice placed her turban on her head, and they awaited the last summons.

In the meantime, Giacomo and Bernardo, whose sentences had been read to them, awaited also the moment of their death. About ten o'clock the members of the Confraternity of Mercy, a Florentine order, arrived at the prison of Tordinona, and halted on the threshold with the crucifix, awaiting the appearance of the unhappy youths. Here a serious accident had nearly happened. As many persons were at the prison windows to see the prisoners come out, someone accidentally threw down a large flower-pot full of earth, which fell into the street and narrowly missed one of the Confraternity who was amongst the torch-bearers just before the crucifix. It passed so close to the torch as to extinguish the flame in its descent.

At this moment the gates opened, and Giacomo appeared first on the threshold. He fell on his knees, adoring the holy crucifix with great devotion. He was completely covered with a large mourning cloak, under which his bare breast was prepared to be torn by the red-hot pincers of the executioner, which were lying ready in a chafing-dish fixed to the cart.

Having ascended the vehicle, in which the executioner placed him so as more readily to perform this office, Bernardo came out, and was thus addressed on his appearance by the fiscal of Rome—

"Signor Bernardo Cenci, in the name of our blessed Redeemer, our Holy Father the Pope spares your life; with the sole condition that you accompany your relatives to the scaffold and to their death, and never forget to pray for those with whom you were condemned to die."

At this unexpected intelligence, a loud murmur of joy spread among the crowd, and the members of the Confraternity immediately untied the small mask which covered the youth's eyes; for, owing to his tender age, it had been thought proper to conceal the scaffold from his sight.

Then the executioner; having disposed of Giacomo, came down from the cart to take Bernardo; whose pardon being formally communicated to him, he took off his handcuffs, and placed him alongside his brother, covering him up with a magnificent cloak embroidered with gold, for the neck and shoulders of the poor lad had been already bared, as a preliminary to his decapitation. People were surprised to see such a rich cloak in the possession of the executioner, but were told that it was the one given by Beatrice to Marzio to pledge him to the murder of her father, which fell to the executioner as a perquisite after the execution of the assassin. The sight of the great assemblage of people produced such an effect upon the boy that he fainted.

The procession then proceeded to the prison of Corte

Savella, marching to the sound of funeral chants. At its gates the sacred crucifix halted for the women to join: they soon appeared, fell on their knees, and worshipped the holy symbol as the others had done. The march to the scaffold was then resumed.

The two female prisoners followed the last row of penitents in single file, veiled to the waist, with the distinction that Lucrezia, as a widow, wore a black veil and high-heeled slippers of the same hue, with bows of ribbon, as was the fashion; whilst Beatrice, as a young unmarried girl, wore a silk flat cap to match her corsage, with a plush hood, which fell over her shoulders and covered her violet frock; white slippers with high heels, ornamented with gold rosettes and cherry-coloured fringe. The arms of both were untrammelled, except far a thin slack cord which left their hands free to carry a crucifix and a handkerchief.

During the night a lofty scaffold had been erected on the bridge of Sant' Angelo, and the plank and block were placed thereon. Above the block was hung, from a large cross beam, a ponderous axe, which, guided by two grooves, fell with its whole weight at the touch of a spring.

In this formation the procession wended its way towards the bridge of Sant' Angela. Lucrezia, the more broken down of the two, wept bitterly; but Beatrice was firm and unmoved. On arriving at the open space before the bridge, the women were led into a chapel, where they were shortly joined by Giacomo and Bernardo; they remained together for a few moments, when the brothers were led away to the scaffold, although one was to be executed last, and the other was pardoned. But when they had mounted the platform, Bernardo fainted a second time; and as the executioner was approaching to his assistance, some of the crowd, supposing that his object was to decapitate him, cried loudly, "He is pardoned!" The executioner reassured them by seating Bernardo near the block, Giacomo kneeling on the other side.

Then the executioner descended, entered the chapel, and reappeared leading Lucrezia, who was the first to suffer. At the foot of the scaffold he tied her hands behind her back, tore open the top of her corsage so as to uncover her shoulders, gave her the crucifix to kiss, and led her to the step ladder, which she ascended with great difficulty, on account of her extreme stoutness; then, on her reaching the platform, he removed the veil which covered her head. On this exposure of her features to the immense crowd, Lucrezia shuddered from head to foot; then, her eyes full of tears, she cried with a loud voice—

"O my God, have mercy upon me; and do you, brethren, pray for my soul!"

Having uttered these words, not knowing what was required of her, she turned to Alessandro, the chief executioner, and asked what she was to do; he told her to bestride the plank and lie prone upon it; which she did with great trouble and timidity; but as she was unable, on account of the fullness of her bust, to lay her neck upon the block, this had to be raised by placing a billet of wood underneath it; all this time the poor woman, suffering even more from shame than from fear, was kept in suspense; at length, when she was properly adjusted, the executioner touched the spring, the knife fell, and the decapitated head, falling on the platform of the scaffold, bounded two or three times in the air, to the general horror; the executioner then seized it, showed it to the multitude, and wrapping it in black taffetas, placed it with the body on a bier at the foot of the scaffold.

Whilst arrangements were being made for the decapitation of Beatrice, several stands, full of spectators, broke down; some people were killed by this accident, and still more lamed and injured.

The machine being now rearranged and washed, the executioner returned to the chapel to take charge of Beatrice, who, on seeing the sacred crucifix, said some prayers for her soul, and on her hands being tied, cried out, "God grant that you be binding this body unto corruption, and loosing this soul unto life eternal!" She then arose, proceeded to the platform, where she devoutly kissed the stigmata; then leaving her slippers at the foot of the scaffold, she nimbly ascended the ladder, and instructed beforehand, promptly lay down on the plank, without exposing her naked shoulders. But her precautions to shorten the bitterness of death were of no avail, for the pope, knowing her impetuous disposition, and fearing lest she might be led into the commission of some sin between absolution and death, had given orders that the moment Beatrice was extended on the scaffold a signal gun should be fired from the castle of Sant' Angelo;

which was done, to the great astonishment of everybody, including Beatrice herself, who, not expecting this explosion, raised herself almost upright; the pope meanwhile, who was praying at Monte Cavallo, gave her absolution 'in articulo mortis'. About five minutes thus passed, during which the sufferer waited with her head replaced on the block; at length, when the executioner judged that the absolution had been given, he released the spring, and the axe fell.

A gruesome sight was then afforded: whilst the head bounced away on one side of the block, on the other the body rose erect, as if about to step backwards; the executioner exhibited the head, and disposed of it and the body as before. He wished to place Beatrice's body with that of her stepmother, but the brotherhood of Mercy took it out of his hands, and as one of them was attempting to lay it on the bier, it slipped from him and fell from the scaffold to the ground below; the dress being partially torn from the body, which was so besmeared with dust and blood that much time was occupied in washing it. Poor Bernardo was so overcome by this horrible scene that he swooned away for the third time, and it was necessary to revive him with stimulants to witness the fate of his elder brother.

The turn of Giacomo at length arrived: he had witnessed the death of his stepmother and his sister, and his clothes were covered with their blood; the executioner approached him and tore off his cloak, exposing his bare breast covered with the wounds caused by the grip of red-hot pincers; in this state, and half-naked, he rose to his feet, and turning to his brother, said—

"Bernardo, if in my examination I have compromised and accused you, I have done so falsely, and although I have already disavowed this declaration, I repeat, at the moment of appearing before God, that you are innocent, and that it is a cruel abuse of justice to compel you to witness this frightful spectacle."

The executioner then made him kneel down, bound his legs to one of the beams erected on the scaffold, and having bandaged his eyes, shattered his head with a blow of his mallet; then, in the sight of all, he hacked his body into four quarters. The official party then left, taking with them Bernardo, who, being in a state of high fever, was bled and put to bed.

The corpses of the two ladies were laid out each on its bier under the statue of St. Paul, at the foot of the bridge, with four torches of white wax, which burned till four o'clock in the afternoon; then, along with the remains of Giacomo, they were taken to the church of San Giovanni Decollato; finally, about nine in the evening, the body of Beatrice, covered with flowers, and attired in the dress worn at her execution, was carried to the church of San Pietro in Montorio, with fifty lighted torches, and followed by the brethren of the order of the Stigmata and all the Franciscan monks in Rome; there, agreeably to her wish, it was buried at the foot of the high altar.

The same evening Signora Lucrezia was interred, as she had desired to be, in the church of San Giorgio di Velobre.

All Rome may be said to have been present at this tragedy, carriages, horses, foot people, and cars crowding as it were upon one another. The day was unfortunately so hot, and the sun so scorching, that many persons fainted, others returned home stricken with fever, and some even died during the night, owing to sunstroke from exposure during the three hours occupied by the execution.

The Tuesday following, the 14th of September; being the Feast of the Holy Cross, the brotherhood of San Marcello, by special licence of the pope, set at liberty the unhappy Bernardo Cenci, with the condition of paying within the year two thousand five hundred Roman crowns to the brotherhood of the most Holy Trinity of Pope Sixtus, as may be found to-day recorded in their archives.

Having now seen the tomb, if you desire to form a more vivid impression of the principal actors in this tragedy than can be derived from a narrative, pay a visit to the Barberini Gallery, where you will see, with five other masterpieces by Guido, the portrait of Beatrice, taken, some say the night before her execution, others during her progress to the scaffold; it is the head of a lovely girl, wearing a headdress composed of a turban with a lappet. The hair is of a rich fair chestnut hue; the dark eyes are moistened with recent tears; a perfectly farmed nose surmounts an infantile mouth; unfortunately, the loss of tone in the picture since it was painted has destroyed the original fair complexion. The age of the subject may be twenty, or perhaps twenty-two years.

Near this portrait is that of Lucrezia Petrani the small

head indicates a person below the middle height; the attributes are those of a Roman matron in her pride; her high complexion, graceful contour, straight nose, black eyebrows, and expression at the same time imperious and voluptuous indicate this character to the life; a smile still seems to linger an the charming dimpled cheeks and perfect mouth mentioned by the chronicler, and her face is exquisitely framed by luxuriant curls falling from her forehead in graceful profusion.

As for Giacomo and Bernardo, as no portraits of them are in existence, we are obliged to gather an idea of their appearance from the manuscript which has enabled us to compile this sanguinary history; they are thus described by the eye-witness of the closing scene—Giacomo was short, well-made and strong, with black hair and beard; he appeared to be about twenty-six years of age.

Poor Bernardo was the image of his sister, so nearly resembling her, that when he mounted the scaffold his long hair and girlish face led people to suppose him to be Beatrice herself: he might be fourteen or fifteen years of age.

The peace of God be with them!